HOLIDAY HISTORY
VALENTINE'S DAY

by Kristine Spanier, MLIS

pogo

Ideas for Parents and Teachers

Pogo Books let children practice reading informational text while introducing them to nonfiction features such as headings, labels, sidebars, maps, and diagrams, as well as a table of contents, glossary, and index.

Carefully leveled text with a strong photo match offers early fluent readers the support they need to succeed.

Before Reading

- "Walk" through the book and point out the various nonfiction features. Ask the student what purpose each feature serves.
- Look at the glossary together. Read and discuss the words.

Read the Book

- Have the child read the book independently.
- Invite him or her to list questions that arise from reading.

After Reading

- Discuss the child's questions. Talk about how he or she might find answers to those questions.
- Prompt the child to think more. Ask: Many people wear red or pink on Valentine's Day. Do you wear special colors on the holidays you celebrate? What are they?

Pogo Books are published by Jump!
5357 Penn Avenue South
Minneapolis, MN 55419
www.jumplibrary.com

Copyright © 2024 Jump!
International copyright reserved in all countries. No part of this book may be reproduced in any form without written permission from the publisher.

Library of Congress Cataloging-in-Publication Data

Names: Spanier, Kristine, author.
Title: Valentine's Day / by Kristine Spanier, MLIS.
Description: Minneapolis, MN: Jump!, Inc., [2024]
Series: Holiday history | Includes index.
Audience: Ages 7-10
Identifiers: LCCN 2022046209 (print)
LCCN 2022046210 (ebook)
ISBN 9798885244664 (hardcover)
ISBN 9798885244671 (paperback)
ISBN 9798885244688 (ebook)
Subjects: LCSH: Valentine's Day–Juvenile literature.
Valentine's Day–History–Juvenile literature.
Classification: LCC GT4925 .S63 2024 (print)
LCC GT4925 (ebook)
DDC 394.2618–dc23/eng/20220928
LC record available at https://lccn.loc.gov/2022046209
LC ebook record available at https://lccn.loc.gov/2022046210

Editor: Jenna Gleisner
Designer: Molly Ballanger

Photo Credits: Shutterstock, cover, 8-9; Roman Samborskyi/Shutterstock, 1; Marina Burrascano/Shutterstock, 3; Sewcream/iStock, 4; Stefania Valvola/Shutterstock, 5; North Wind Picture Archives/Alamy, 6-7; iStock, 8-9; lisegagne/iStock, 10-11; Sokor Space/Shutterstock, 12; Jose Luis Pelaez Inc/Getty, 13; Liliboas/iStock, 14-15; MR.VICHIT LAMOOL/Shutterstock, 16; RONALDO SCHEMIDT/Getty, 17; REUTERS/Alamy, 18-19; kirin_photo/iStock, 20-21; JeniFoto/Shutterstock, 23.

Printed in the United States of America at Corporate Graphics in North Mankato, Minnesota.

TABLE OF CONTENTS

CHAPTER 1
A Day for Love 4

CHAPTER 2
Valentine's Day Traditions 12

CHAPTER 3
Valentine's Day Around the World 16

QUICK FACTS & TOOLS
Valentine's Day Place of Origin 22
Quick Facts 22
Glossary 23
Index 24
To Learn More 24

CHAPTER 1
A DAY FOR LOVE

Have you ever given someone a **valentine**? Valentines are a way to show love. People have been sending them since the 1400s. How did this **tradition** and Valentine's Day begin? People do not know for sure!

One story tells of a man named Valentine. He lived in the 200s. It is said that he healed sick children. He also helped people get married. He died on February 14. The **Catholic Church** named the date Valentine's Day.

The first valentines were made by hand in England. People wrote poems on them. In the late 1700s, **printing presses** began making them. They became more popular.

In 1840, Great Britain began the **penny post**. Anyone could mail a card for just one penny. Around 400,000 valentines were sent the next year.

WHAT DO YOU THINK?

Today, 25 million valentines are sent in Great Britain every year. In the United States, 145 million valentines are sent! Do you think people should send valentines? Why or why not?

valentine

People in the United States began sending cards in the mid-1800s. Some were for friends or family. Others were **romantic**. Many said "Be my Valentine."

WHAT DO YOU THINK?

Valentines often show Cupid. This is the Roman god of love. According to **myths**, whoever Cupid hits with his arrows falls in love! Have you seen images of Cupid? Where were they?

Valentine's Day parties began in the 1700s in England. People played games. They drew names from boxes to choose valentines. They gave their valentines presents. Gloves were a popular gift for women!

> **DID YOU KNOW?**
>
> Geoffrey Chaucer wrote a love poem in the late 1300s. It describes birds choosing **mates** on Valentine's Day. William Shakespeare wrote plays in the late 1500s and early 1600s. Some mentioned Valentine's Day. These writings helped connect Valentine's Day to love.

CHAPTER 1

CHAPTER 2
VALENTINE'S DAY TRADITIONS

People still show **affection** by exchanging cards and gifts on Valentine's Day. At school, students often trade valentines. They decorate special boxes or bags to put them in.

Families celebrate the holiday, too. Some make valentines or treats. Others share a special meal.

Many couples go on dates. They might dress in red or pink. Some exchange valentines. Flowers, candy, and jewelry are popular gifts.

TAKE A LOOK!

Red, pink, and white are colors and **symbols** of Valentine's Day. What are some other Valentine's Day symbols? Take a look!

HEARTS

LOVEBIRDS

CUPID

ROSES

JEWELRY

CHOCOLATES

CHAPTER 2

15

CHAPTER 3
VALENTINE'S DAY AROUND THE WORLD

People around the world celebrate Valentine's Day. In England, some give teddy bears to loved ones. Others give a single red rose.

In Mexico, the holiday is known as the Day of Love and Friendship. People gift balloons. Some are shaped like hearts. Many have words about love on them.

CHAPTER 3

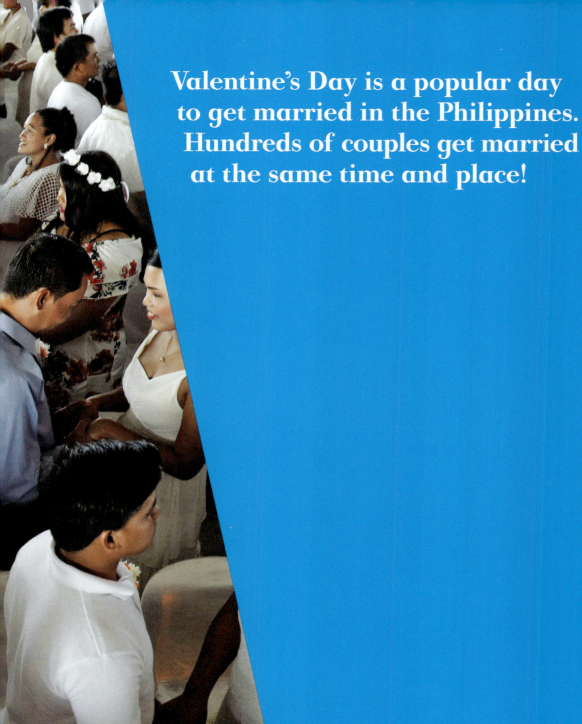

Valentine's Day is a popular day to get married in the Philippines. Hundreds of couples get married at the same time and place!

CHAPTER 3

Valentine's Day is a holiday for affection and love. It is also a day for cards and candy! Will you give someone a valentine on February 14?

CHAPTER 3

QUICK FACTS & TOOLS

VALENTINE'S DAY PLACE OF ORIGIN

QUICK FACTS

Date: February 14

Time of Origin: 1400s

Place of Origin: England

Common Symbols: hearts, red roses, chocolates, lovebirds, Cupid, jewelry, the colors red, pink, and white

Foods: heart-shaped treats, conversation hearts, chocolates, other candy

Traditions: sending valentines, sharing meals with loved ones, making treats, giving gifts, wearing red or pink clothing, going on dates

GLOSSARY

affection: Love for someone or something familiar to you.

Catholic Church: A Christian church that has the pope as its leader.

mates: Each of the partners of a pair of animals.

myths: Old stories that express the beliefs or history of a group of people.

penny post: A postal system in which a letter can be sent for one penny.

printing presses: Large machines that print words and designs by pressing sheets of paper against a surface, such as a metal plate, that has ink on it.

romantic: Of or having to do with love or romance.

symbols: Objects or designs that stand for, suggest, or represent something else.

tradition: A custom, idea, or belief that is handed down from one generation to the next.

valentine: A gift or greeting card sent to a loved one on Valentine's Day. A valentine can also refer to a sweetheart or loved one chosen on Valentine's Day.

INDEX

balloons 17
candy 14, 15, 20
card 6, 9, 12, 20
Catholic Church 5
Chaucer, Geoffrey 10
colors 14, 15
Cupid 9, 15
England 6, 10, 16
games 10
gift 10, 12, 14, 16, 17
hearts 15, 17
jewelry 14, 15
love 4, 9, 10, 17, 20
married 5, 19
Mexico 17
parties 10
Philippines 19
poems 6, 10
roses 15, 16
Shakespeare, William 10
symbols 15
teddy bears 16
tradition 4
United States 6, 9
valentine 4, 6, 9, 10, 12, 13, 14, 20
Valentine 5

TO LEARN MORE

Finding more information is as easy as 1, 2, 3.

❶ Go to www.factsurfer.com
❷ Enter "Valentine'sDay" into the search box.
❸ Choose your book to see a list of websites.